South Carolina

BY ANN HEINRICHS

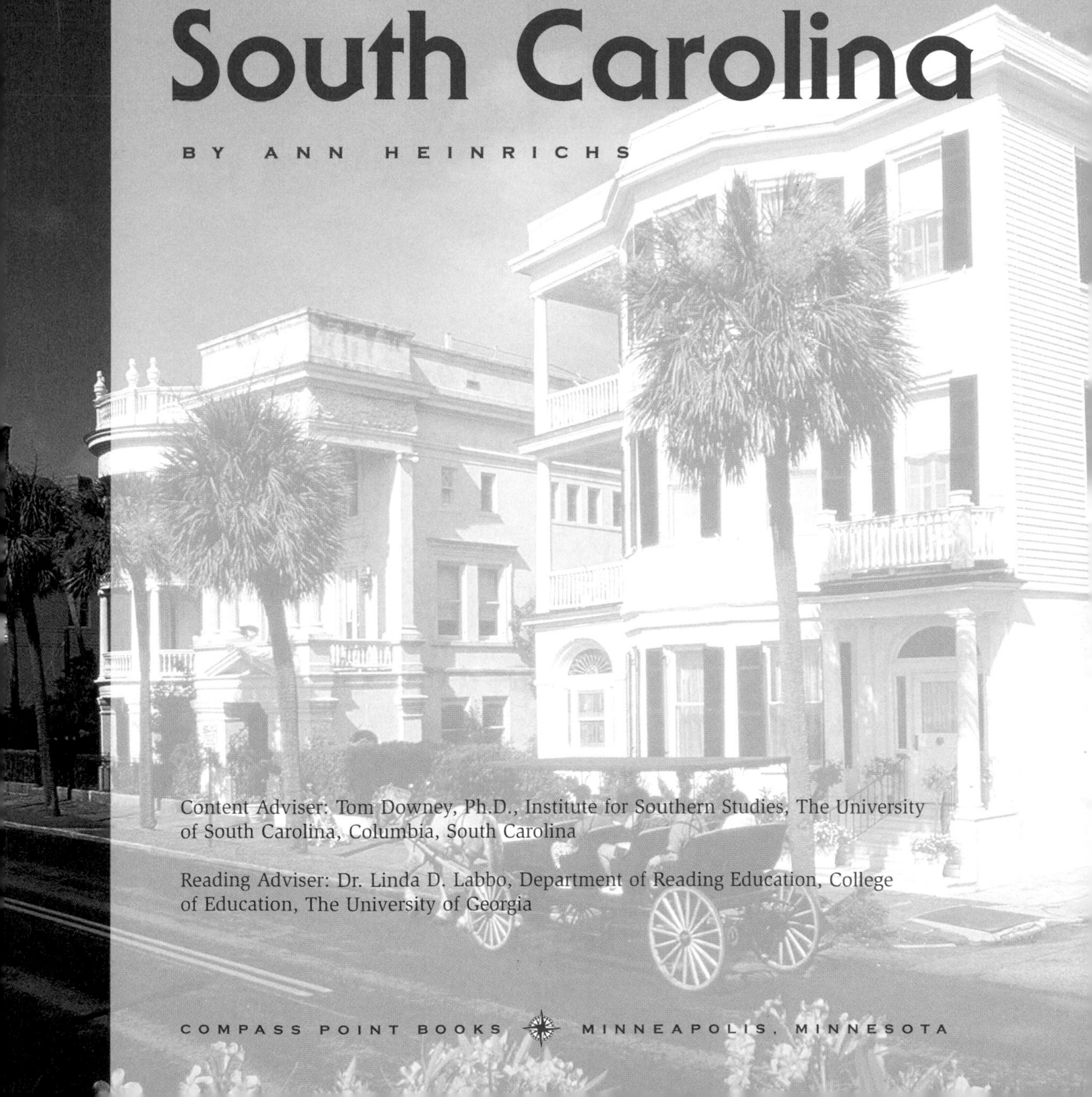

Content Adviser: Tom Downey, Ph.D., Institute for Southern Studies, The University of South Carolina, Columbia, South Carolina

Reading Adviser: Dr. Linda D. Labbo, Department of Reading Education, College of Education, The University of Georgia

COMPASS POINT BOOKS

MINNEAPOLIS, MINNESOTA

Compass Point Books
3109 West 50th Street, #115
Minneapolis, MN 55410

Visit Compass Point Books on the Internet at www.compasspointbooks.com
or e-mail your request to custserv@compasspointbooks.com

On the cover: A horse-drawn carriage in front of historic houses in Charleston.

Photographs ©: Bob Krist/Corbis, cover, 1, 12, 28, 31; Gary W. Carter/Visuals Unlimited, 3, 11; Scott Berner/Visuals Unlimited, 5; Peter Johnson/Corbis, 6; Unicorn Stock Photos/Joseph L. Fontenot, 7, 48; John Elk III, 9, 23, 35, 37, 41, 43 (top) 45; Mark E. Gibson/The Image Finders, 10, 47; Stock Montage, 13; North Wind Picture Archives, 14, 15; Library of Congress, 17; Hulton/Archive by Getty Images, 18, 21, 29, 46; Bettmann/Corbis, 19; Michael T. Sedam/Corbis, 20; Unicorn Stock Photos/Robin Rudd, 24; Corbis, 25; Brownie Harris/Corbis, 26; Unicorn Stock Photos/Jeff Greenberg, 27; Matthew Mendelsohn/ Corbis, 30; Michael DeMocker/Visuals Unlimited, 32; Patti McConville/The Image Finders, 33; Craig Jones/Getty Images, 34; Annie Griffiths Belt/Corbis, 36; Unicorn Stock Photos/Robert W. Ginn, 39; www.dlawrence.com, 40; Tom Till, 42; Robesus, Inc, 43 (state flag); One Mile Up, Inc, 43 (state seal); Hal Horwitz/Corbis, 44 (top left); Bill Leaman/The Image Finders, 44 (middle left); Unicorn Stock Photos/Gary Randall, 44 (bottom left); Comstock, 44 (bottom right).

Editors: E. Russell Primm, Emily J. Dolbear, and Catherine Neitge
Photo Researcher: Svetlana Zhurkina
Photo Selector: Linda S. Koutris
Designer: The Design Lab
Cartographer: XNR Productions, Inc.

Library of Congress Cataloging-in-Publication Data

Heinrichs, Ann.
    South Carolina / by Ann Heinrichs.
       p. cm. — (This land is your land)
    Summary: Introduces the geography, history, government, people, culture, and attractions of South Carolina. Includes bibliographical references and index.
    ISBN 0-7565-0326-4 (hardcover)
    1. South Carolina—Juvenile literature. [1. South Carolina.] I. Title.
    F269.3 .H45 2003
    975.7—dc21
                                                                    2002010105

Table of Contents

4 Welcome to South Carolina!

6 Mountains, Plains, and Coasts

13 A Trip Through Time

21 Government by the People

25 South Carolinians at Work

29 Getting to Know South Carolinians

35 Let's Explore South Carolina!

41 Important Dates

42 Glossary

42 Did You Know?

43 At a Glance

44 State Symbols

44 Making Biscuits and Gravy

45 State Songs

46 Famous South Carolinians

47 Want to Know More?

48 Index

Welcome to South Carolina!

William Bartram was a scientist who studied nature. He traveled through South Carolina in the 1770s. In his journal, he wrote about this beautiful land.

Bartram saw "vast forests, . . . delightful strawberry plains, and gently swelling green hills." There were "steep and rocky ridges" and rivers "speeding through the lucid green plain." The soil was "exceedingly fertile."

This fertile soil once supported huge rice and cotton plantations. Reminders of that time can be seen today. Many large plantation houses are still standing. Later, South Carolina's swift rivers provided power for factories. The state became a leader in making textiles, or cloth. Textiles are still a leading industry. South Carolina also produces chemicals, paper, and many farm products.

Visitors still enjoy the natural beauty that Bartram saw. They love the state's mountains, forests, and sandy beaches. They watch deer, foxes, sea turtles, alligators, and dolphins. Now let's see what you like best about South Carolina!

▲ South Carolina is known for its rolling hills and fertile soil.

Mountains, Plains, and Coasts

South Carolina is one of America's southern states. On the east, it faces the Atlantic Ocean. To the north is North Carolina. Georgia lies to the south and west, across the Savannah River.

South Carolina is shaped like a slice of pizza. Its pointed tip is in the west. Western South Carolina is part of what is called the up country. It's in the Appalachian Mountains.

▶ Swamp cypresses reflect in the flooded waters of the Savannah River.

▲ Table Rock Mountain in the Blue Ridge Mountains

The Blue Ridge Mountains rise in the far northwest. East of the mountains is the hilly Piedmont region. Greenville and Spartanburg are major industrial cities here. The Piedmont's many rivers rush to the southeast. They tumble over a sharp drop called the Fall Line that runs across the middle of the state.

Eastern South Carolina—the Coastal Plain—covers more than half the state. South Carolinians call this the low country. Its rich soil is great for farming. Sand hills run along the base of the Fall Line. Long ago, the ocean reached inland to this point. The sand hills were once ocean beaches.

▶ **A topographic map of South Carolina**

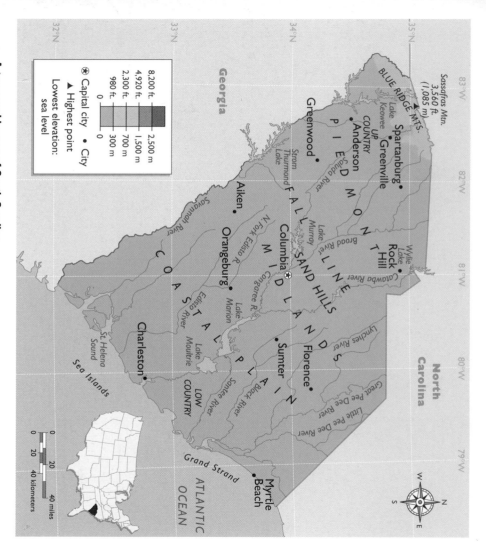

Georgia

North Carolina

BLUE RIDGE MTS.

Sassafras Mtn.
3,560 ft.
(1,085 m)

35°N

34°N

33°N

32°N

83°W 82°W 81°W 80°W 79°W

Elevation	
8,200 ft.	2,500 m
4,920 ft.	1,500 m
2,300 ft.	700 m
980 ft.	300 m
0	0

⊛ Capital city • City
▲ Highest point
Lowest elevation: sea level

Lake Keowee
UP COUNTRY
Spartanburg
Greenville
Anderson
Greenwood

P I E D M O N T

Strom Thurmond Lake
Saluda River
Lake Murray
Broad River
Catawba River
Lake Wylie
Rock Hill

F A L L   L I N E

S A N D   H I L L S

Savannah River
Aiken
Orangeburg
N. Fork Edisto R.
Columbia ⊛
Congaree R.
Wateree River
M I D L A N D S
Lynches River
Florence
Sumter
Great Pee Dee River
Little Pee Dee River

C O A S T A L   P L A I N

Edisto River
Lake Marion
Lake Moultrie
Santee River
Black River
LOW COUNTRY
St. Helena Sound
Sea Islands
Charleston

Grand Strand
Myrtle Beach

ATLANTIC OCEAN

N W E S

0 20 40 miles
0 20 40 kilometers

▲ Many grand homes still line the port city of Charleston.

Closer to the coast, the land becomes swampy, or wet. Charleston and its busy port face the Atlantic Ocean. Sandy beaches stretch along the northern coast. This strip is called the Grand Strand. Myrtle Beach is a popular vacation destination in this area. Farther south, dozens of islands lie offshore. The Sea Islands hug the coast south of Charleston.

Forests cover more than half the state. They shelter deer, wild turkeys, foxes, and raccoons. Thick Spanish moss hangs down from oaks and cypresses along the coast.

► Spanish moss hangs from a live oak tree.

▲ South Carolina's swamps support a variety of plant and animal life.

The graceful palmetto, the state tree, grows near the coast. It is a type of palm tree. The **swamps** are home to alligators, bears, and waterbirds. Dolphins, sharks, and sea turtles live in the waters along the coast.

▶ An egret wades near a Charleston garden blooming with azaleas.

Some people visit South Carolina in the winter. They enjoy the low-lands and the sandy beaches. The western mountains can get pretty cold, though. Sweet smells fill the air in the spring. Gardens throughout the state are in bloom. Summers in South Carolina are very warm and sunny. The central part of the state gets the warmest weather.

A Trip Through Time

Many American Indians once lived in South Carolina. The Catawba people farmed, hunted, and fished. Their round, bark-covered homes stood near the Catawba River. The Cherokee lived in large farming villages to the west. They made their homes of woven branches and mud. They held meetings and religious ceremonies in large council houses. The Yamasee lived in the southeast. Dozens of other groups lived in South Carolina, too. The names of several Native American groups live on in modern place names. For instance, the Edisto, the Pee Dee, and the Combahee Rivers take their names from Indian groups.

The Spanish explorer Hernando de Soto arrived around 1540. He destroyed many American Indian villages along his path. People from England settled at Albemarle Point in 1670. This became Charleston, the oldest city in South Carolina.

▲ **Hernando de Soto**

This area was in Britain's Carolina **Colony**. In 1729, Carolina split into North Carolina and South Carolina. Planters built huge rice and **indigo** plantations. Using force, they brought African slaves to work their fields. In many plantation areas, slaves far outnumbered the white people living there. Slavery made large plantation farming possible. Farming and trade made South Carolina a rich colony. Without slaves to work the plantations, South Carolina would not have been so rich.

TO BE SOLD by William

Yeomans, (in Charles Town Merchants,) a parcel of good Plantation Slaves. Encouragements will be given by selling Rice in Payment, or any leg saddles and Furniture, choice Barbados and Boston Rum, also Cordial Waters and Limejuice, as well as a parcel of extraordinary Indian trading Goods, and many of other sorts suitable for the Season.

A Time Credit, Security is to be given if required There's likewise to be sold, very Good Troop-

▶ An advertisement for a slave auction in the Charleston Gazette

Over time, the colonists began to wish for freedom. They no longer wanted to be ruled by a king from across the ocean. They fought the British in the Revolutionary War (1775–1783). Many important battles took place in South Carolina. Colonists won battles at Sullivan's Island, Kings Mountain, and Cowpens. After many years of fighting, the

▲ The colonists defeated the British in the Battle of Sullivan's Island in 1776.

American colonies won their freedom. South Carolina became the eighth U.S. state in 1788.

South Carolinians felt strongly about their rights. They believed the U.S. government's **tariffs**, or trade taxes, hurt their economy. In 1832, the state passed an act of **nullification.** It said the tariff laws didn't have to be obeyed. South Carolina was the only state to make the argument for nullification. President Andrew Jackson—a South Carolina native—said that South Carolina had to obey the tariff laws. After some tense talks, South Carolina backed down and paid the tariffs.

South Carolinians also believed in their right to own slaves. They feared the federal government would outlaw slavery. In 1860, the state seceded, or separated itself from the Union. Ten Southern states soon followed its lead. Together, they formed the Confederate States of America. On April 12, 1861, Confederate troops fired on Fort Sumter in Charleston. This started the Civil War (1861–1865).

As a result of the war, the slaves were freed at last. It would be a long time, however, before they enjoyed their rights as citizens. For decades, African-Americans were

▲ The Civil War started when the Confederate army attacked Fort Sumter.

segregated, or separated, from whites. Most could not vote. They had to attend separate schools that were not as good as the schools for white people. They could get only the lowest-paying jobs. **Segregation** would not come to an end until the 1960s.

The Civil War had left South Carolina in ruins. Many cities and farms were destroyed.

▶ The wreckage of Columbia after Union forces swept through it

In the early twentieth century, South Carolina became a leader in making cotton cloth. Busy textile mills sprang up in the Piedmont region. They used that area's abundant water power to run the textile machinery. Factory owners designed and built many mill villages. They wanted to attract workers to the mills and give them a place to live once they arrived. As many as one in every six white South Carolinians lived in a mill village by the 1920s. Like the rest of South Carolina, mill villages were strictly segregated, and most mill jobs were reserved for whites only.

Insects called boll weevils swept through the state. They destroyed much of South Carolina's cotton crop in the 1920s. Then, in the 1930s, the Great Depression hit the United States hard. Thousands of people lost their homes, their farms, and their jobs.

▲ Farm workers in the 1930s

South Carolina's beaches are popular with tourists.

During World War II (1939–1945), South Carolina had many military bases. By the 1960s, African-Americans began to gain equality. They were finally able to vote, attend the same schools as whites, and get better-paying jobs. They could live and shop wherever they chose. Many new factories helped the state's economy grow.

Today, both industry and agriculture are important parts of South Carolina's economy. Tourism also plays an important role. Many people visit the state to enjoy its mountains, its beaches, and its historic sites.

Government by the People

South Carolina is proud of its leaders. Andrew Jackson was probably born in Waxhaw Settlement, near the border with North Carolina. He became the seventh U.S. president in 1829. John C. Calhoun led the fight for states' rights. He served the nation as secretary of war, secretary of state, senator, and as vice president from 1825 to 1832. James Byrnes was a U.S. representative and a senator in the 1920s and 1930s. He also served as a U.S. Supreme Court justice and was secretary of state under President Harry Truman. During the 1930s and 1940s, Byrnes was also an important adviser to President Franklin D. Roosevelt. Strom Thurmond joined the U.S. Senate in 1955 and served longer than any other senator. He did not seek reelection in 2002, the year he turned 100!

▲ **Senator Strom Thurmond**

South Carolina's state government is much like the U.S. government. It is divided into three branches—legislative, executive, and judicial.

The legislative branch makes the state laws. It also decides how the state will spend its money. Voters elect their lawmakers to serve in the general assembly. It has two

▶ **A geopolitical map of South Carolina**

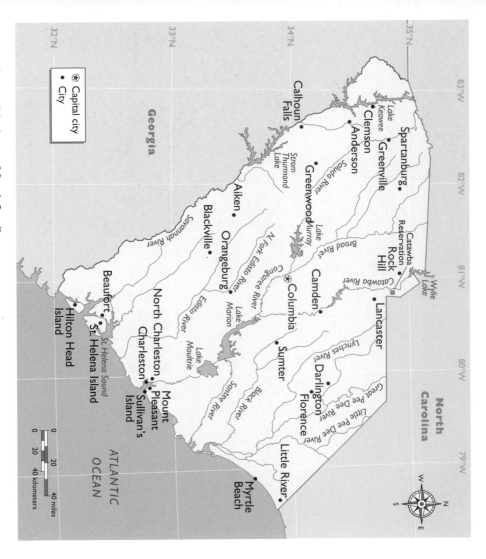

Capital city
City

North Carolina

Georgia

ATLANTIC OCEAN

35°N
34°N
33°N
32°N

83°W
82°W
81°W
80°W
79°W

Catawba Reservation
Rock Hill
Wylie Lake
Catawba River
Lancaster
Sumter
Darlington
Florence
Little River
Myrtle Beach
Great Pee Dee River
Little Pee Dee River
Lynches River
Black River
Santee River
Lake Moultrie
Lake Marion
Camden
Columbia
Broad River
Lake Murray
Saluda River
Congaree River
Edisto River
N. Fork Edisto River
Orangeburg
Blackville
Aiken
Greenwood
Strom Thurmond Lake
Savannah River
Anderson
Clemson
Lake Keowee
Greenville
Spartanburg
Calhoun Falls
Beaufort
Hilton Head Island
St. Helena Island
St. Helena Sound
North Charleston
Charleston
Mount Pleasant
Sullivan's Island

0   20   40 miles
0   20   40 kilometers

N W E S

▲ **The South Carolina State House**

houses, or parts. One is the 46-member senate. The other is the 124-member house of representatives. The general assembly meets in the South Carolina State House in Columbia, the capital city.

The executive branch makes sure the state's laws are carried out. South Carolina's governor heads the executive branch. Voters choose a governor every four years. Voters also elect eight other executive officers. They include the lieutenant governor and the attorney general.

The judicial branch is made up of judges and courts. The judges know a lot about South Carolina's laws. They decide whether someone has broken the law. South Carolina's highest court is the supreme court. Its five judges are elected by the general assembly.

South Carolina is divided into forty-six counties. Voters elect people to serve on county commissions or councils. These officers take care of county government. Cities and towns elect city councils and mayors or managers.

▶ Local governments help build things such as this town square in Abbeville.

South Carolinians at Work

Farming was once South Carolina's biggest business. Huge plantations grew cotton, rice, indigo, and tobacco. By 1930, the state's textile mills led the nation. Today, manufacturing is the leading industry. Many factories are in the Greenville, Spartanburg, and Anderson areas.

▲ A South Carolina cotton farmer in 1938

▶ **Employees working in a textile mill**

South Carolina is still a top textile-producing state. Its mills make cloth, thread, yarn, and finished clothing. Chemicals, however, are the leading factory products. They include plastics, dyes, medicines, and **artificial** fibers. South Carolina also makes motor vehicles and parts. Other factory goods include computers, foods, and machines. Forests cover much of the state. Their trees are made into many wood and paper products.

South Carolina's farms are still going strong. Broilers are the state's top farm products. They are chickens from five to twelve weeks old. Next in importance are plants for people's homes and gardens. These include flowers, shrubs, and trees. Tobacco, turkeys, cattle, and cotton are next in value.

▲ A South Carolina chicken house

Granite and limestone are leading minerals in South Carolina. Granite is strong and becomes shiny when polished. As a result, it is prized as a building stone. Just look at the State House in Columbia. Most of its granite came from near-by Granby. South Carolina also mines a lot of kaolin—a clay used for making pottery and dishes.

Most South Carolina workers hold service jobs. Instead of producing goods, they provide helpful services. They may sell cars or food. Some are tour guides or hotel workers. Others work in military bases, schools, hospitals, or banks.

▶ South Carolina's service workers include the friendly staff of this Charleston hotel.

Getting to Know South Carolinians

Many gifted people have come from South Carolina. They include trumpeter Dizzy Gillespie and singer Eartha Kitt. DuBose Heyward wrote the novel *Porgy* (1925). In 1935, it was turned into the opera *Porgy and Bess.*

▲ **Jazz musician Dizzy Gillespie**

Julia Peterkin wrote about the lives of slaves on plantations. One of her books, *Scarlet Sister Mary* (1928), won the 1929 Pulitzer Prize. Several of Pat Conroy's novels were made into movies. They include *The Prince of Tides* (1986) and *The Great Santini* (1976). James Dickey is a well-known poet. Jasper Johns is famous for his pop art paintings.

South Carolina is a small state, but more than 4 million people lived there in 2000. Columbia, the capital of South Carolina, is also its largest city. Other large cities are Charleston, North Charleston, and Greenville.

▲ **A drummer at the Gullah Festival in Beaufort**

For much of South Carolina's early history, African slaves made up more than half the population. Today, almost one of every three residents is African-American. The Sea Islands have a rich black **culture.** Some people there speak *Gullah,* a blend of English and West African languages. This Gullah culture has almost disappeared in recent years. Many people are now working to save it, especially at the Penn Center on Saint Helena Island and at the College of Charleston.

Many white South Carolinians are descended from early settlers. They have roots in England, Scotland, Ireland, or France. The Catawba are the largest Native American group. Their **reservation** is near Lancaster.

A shrimp boat in South Carolina

Springtime is flower time in South Carolina. Garden tours go on all over the state. Mount Pleasant celebrates its shrimp industry in April. It begins with the Blessing of the Fleet, when a minister blesses the shrimp boats. That kicks off the big Seafood Festival.

Charleston's Spoleto Festival is a grand event in May. Hundreds of actors, singers, and dancers put on shows there. Beaufort's Gullah Festival celebrates the Sea Islands' culture. It's a time for African music, dance, and storytelling. June brings the Sun Fun Festival to Myrtle Beach. The Watermelon Festival in Hampton is said to be the state's oldest. Irmo holds the Okra Strut, and Batesburg-Leesville holds an annual Poultry Festival. And don't miss the South Carolina State Fair held in Columbia in October.

▲ **The Citadel, a military college in South Carolina**

The College of Charleston, Clemson University, and the University of South Carolina (USC) are major colleges. Near Charleston is The Citadel. Its full name is the Military College of South Carolina.

Football season is an exciting time for South Carolinians. They go wild over their college football teams. The Clemson Tigers are big-time favorites. The Fighting Gamecocks are USC's football champs. The annual Clemson–USC football game is the biggest rivalry in the state. They have played each other almost every year since 1896.

Golfers love playing on Hilton Head Island and the Grand Strand. Car racing is a popular sport, too. The Southern 500 is held in Darlington every Labor Day weekend. It is one of the biggest auto-racing events in the United States.

Horse racing also has its share of fans. Camden holds the Carolina Cup and the Colonial Cup. Both are steeplechase races, competitions in which horses jump over fences and walls. Aiken hosts its own "Triple Crown" every spring. It holds a traditional horse race, a steeplechase, and a harness race.

Let's Explore South Carolina

What was life like in the plantation days? Visit Charleston, and you're sure to get a clue. Parts of Charleston seem frozen in time. Ride a horse-drawn carriage along the cobblestone streets. You'll see many huge homes from the 1700s and 1800s. In Charleston Harbor, you can visit Fort Sumter. Here the first shots of the Civil War rang out.

▲ The Edmonston-Alston House, a historic home in Charleston

▶ A majestic heron of the
Sea Islands

Many plantation sites stand near Charleston. Drayton Hall was built around 1740. It is an excellent example of **Georgian** architecture. Middleton Place is the site of the oldest sculpted gardens in the United States.

Along the coast are beaches, sand dunes, and swamps. Myrtle Beach and Hilton Head Island are popular vacation spots. Away from the crowds, you'll discover nature. Long-legged herons spear fish with their bills. Sea turtles nest on the shore. Gullah culture can be found on the Sea Islands. Saint Helena Island's Museum explores its crafts and folklore.

South Carolinians are proud of the State House in Columbia.

▲ **A view of Union cannonball damage to South Carolina's State House**

It was only half built during the Civil War. You can still see where cannonballs hit its walls. About one-third of Columbia was destroyed by the war. The South Carolina State Museum brings history and science to life. There you can walk beneath a giant shark. You'll see dinosaur fossils. You'll learn how **lasers** work, too. Dr. Charles Townes, the "father" of the laser, is from South Carolina. Riverbanks Zoo is in Columbia, too. Its animals enjoy their natural habitats.

Greenville became a leading textile center by the start of the twentieth century. Swift rivers gave power to its many textile mills. Now Greenville and Spartanburg are

▶ **Places to visit in South Carolina**

busy factory centers. This area has attracted industries from around the world, especially Japan and Western Europe. Greenville's Nippon Center explores Japanese culture. German BMW cars are made in Greer, near Spartanburg. Visitors can tour the factory.

You know when you're near Gaffney. You can see its

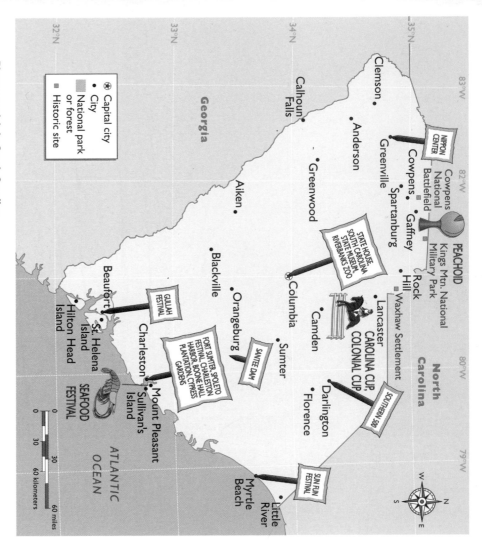

▲ Gaffney's Peachoid

Peachoid from miles away. The Peachoid is a peach-shaped water tower. It lets you know you're in peach-growing country! Gaffney sits between two battlefields. They are Kings Mountain and Cowpens. Colonists fought the British here—and won! Both sites offer programs on their history.

The Cherokee cleared trails through the Blue Ridge

Mountains. Now many of those trails are roads. They wind through the forests, past streams and waterfalls. Sassafras Mountain is the state's highest point. Stand on its peak, and you see four states! They are Tennessee, North Carolina, South Carolina, and Georgia. You can't tell where their borders are, of course. Someone your age probably stood there long ago. There were no states then, but the rolling mountains looked about the same.

Important Dates

1540 Spanish explorer Hernando de Soto arrives in South Carolina.

1670 South Carolina's first permanent English settlement is at Albemarle Point.

1729 South Carolina becomes a separate colony.

1780 Americans win the Battle of Kings Mountain in the Revolutionary War.

1788 South Carolina becomes a state on May 23.

1860 South Carolina secedes from the Union on December 20.

1861 Confederate troops fire on Fort Sumter on April 12, beginning the Civil War.

1865 The Civil War ends.

1895 South Carolina adopts a new constitution.

1920s Boll weevils destroy much of South Carolina's cotton crop.

1953 The Savannah River Plant produces nuclear weapons.

1970 The first African-Americans are elected to the state house of representatives since 1902.

1989 Hurricane Hugo strikes the coastal area on September 21.

1992 South Carolinians elect James E. Clyburn to the U.S. House of Representatives. He becomes the first African-American congressman elected by the state since the 1870s.

Glossary

artificial—human-made; manufactured

colony—a territory that belongs to the country that settles it

culture—a group of beliefs, customs, and a way of life

Georgian—relating to a style popular in Great Britain and the U.S. in the eighteenth and early nineteenth centuries

indigo—a plant used to make a blue dye

lasers—devices that channel radiation into a powerful beam of energy

nullification—declaring a law to be improper and invalid

plantations—large farms worked by laborers who lived there

reservation—large area of land set aside for Native Americans

segregation—the practice of separating whites and blacks

swamps—lands partly covered with water

tariffs—taxes on shipped goods

textiles—cloth

Did You Know?

★ The Carolina Colony was named for Great Britain's King Charles. His name is *Carolus* in Latin.

★ The wood of the palmetto is spongy. British cannonballs bounced off Sullivan Island's palmetto-log fort during the Revolutionary War. As a result, the palmetto became a state symbol.

★ The Reform branch of the Jewish faith in the United States began in Charleston in 1824.

★ Kudzu is a plant pest in western South Carolina. People brought this climbing vine from Japan in 1876. It covers trees until they can get no sunlight and die.

★ South Carolina's Whitewater Falls is the highest waterfall in the eastern United States.

At a Glance

State capital: Columbia

State mottoes: *Animis Opibusque Parati* (Latin for "Prepared in Mind and Resources") and *Dum Spiro Spero* (Latin for "While I Breathe, I Hope")

State nickname: Palmetto State

Statehood: May 23, 1788; eighth state

Area: 31,117 square miles (80,587 sq km); **rank:** fortieth

Highest point: Sassafras Mountain, 3,560 feet (1,085 m) above sea level

Lowest point: Sea level, along the coast

Highest recorded temperature: 111°F (44°C) at Blackville on September 4, 1925; at Calhoun Falls on September 8, 1925; and at Camden on June 28, 1954

Lowest recorded temperature: −19°F (−28°C) at Caesar's Head on January 21, 1985

Average January temperature: 45°F (7°C)

Average July temperature: 80°F (27°C)

Population in 2000: 4,012,012; **rank:** twenty-sixth

Largest cities in 2000: Columbia (116,278), Charleston (96,650), North Charleston (79,641), Greenville (56,002)

Factory products: Chemicals, textiles, motor vehicles, forest products

Farm products: Tobacco, decorative plants, poultry, cotton, cattle

Mining products: Granite, limestone

State flag: South Carolina's state flag shows a palmetto tree and a crescent moon. They are white against a blue background. The palmetto is the state tree. The crescent is the emblem that South Carolina's troops wore on their caps during the Revolutionary War.

State seal: The state seal shows two scenes. On the left is a palmetto over a dead oak. This represents South Carolina's defense against the British in the Battle of Sullivan's Island. South Carolina's fort was built of palmetto logs. The British ships were oak. Around this scene is the state motto that means "Prepared in Mind and Resources." On the right is a woman who stands for hope. She walks along a beach full of swords. This represents hope overcoming danger. Around this scene is the motto that means "While I Breathe, I Hope."

State abbreviations: S.C. (traditional); SC (postal)

State Symbols

State bird: Carolina wren

State flower: Yellow jessamine

State tree: Palmetto

State animal: White-tailed deer

State dog: Boykin spaniel

State wild game bird: Wild turkey

State fish: Striped bass

State reptile: Loggerhead turtle

State insect: Praying mantis (Carolina mantid)

State shell: Lettered olive

State fruit: Peach

State stone: Blue granite

State gemstone: Amethyst

State beverage: Milk

State dance: Shag

State botanical garden: Botanical Garden at Clemson University

State commemorative quarter: released on May 22, 2000

Making Biscuits and Gravy

This is a favorite breakfast meal in South Carolina!

Makes about eighteen biscuits.

INGREDIENTS:

1 3/4 cups flour

3/4 teaspoon salt

2 1/2 teaspoons baking powder

1/3 cup shortening

3/4 cup milk

Canned or homemade gravy

(South Carolinians recommend sausage gravy.)

DIRECTIONS:

Make sure an adult helps with the hot oven. Preheat the oven to 450°.

Mix together the flour, salt, and baking powder. Cut in the shortening. Add the milk and mix. Roll out on a floured board and cut out circles of dough. Place dough circles on a nonstick baking sheet. Bake 'till golden brown, about 12 to 15 minutes. Heat gravy and pour on top of biscuits.

State Songs

"Carolina"

Words by Henry Timrod,
music by Anne Curtis Burgess

Call on thy children of the hill,
Wake swamp and river, coast and rill,
Rouse all thy strength and all thy skill,
Carolina! Carolina!

Hold up the glories of thy dead;
Say how thy elder children bled,
And point to Eutaw's battle-bed,
Carolina! Carolina!

Thy skirts indeed the foe may part,
Thy robe be pierced with sword and dart,
They shall not touch thy noble heart,
Carolina! Carolina!

Throw thy bold banner to the breeze!
Front with thy ranks the threatening seas
Like thine own proud armorial trees,
Carolina! Carolina!

Girt with such wills to do and bear,
Assured in right, and mailed in prayer,
Thou wilt not bow thee to despair,
Carolina! Carolina!

"South Carolina on My Mind"

Words and music by Hank Martin and
Buzz Arledge

At the foot hills of the Appalachian chain,
Down through the rivers, to the
coastal plain,
There's a place that I call home,
And I'll never be alone,
Singin' this Carolina love song.

Chorus:
I've got South Carolina on my mind
Remembering all those sunshine
Summertimes,
And the Autumns in the Smokies when
the leaves turn to gold
Touches my heart and thrills my soul to
have South Carolina on my mind,
With those clean snow-covered mountain
Wintertimes
And the white sand of the beaches and
those Carolina peaches,
I've got South Carolina on my mind.

I'm grown now with a family of my own
In a place that all my kids are callin' home.
And I love this life I'm livin',
And thank God for all He's givin',
But my heart sings a Carolina love song.

Famous South Carolinians

Bernard Baruch (1870–1965) was an adviser to several U.S. presidents, including Woodrow Wilson and Dwight Eisenhower.

Mary McLeod Bethune (1875–1955) fought to provide a good education for African-Americans. She opened a school for girls in Daytona Beach, Florida. Today it's Bethune-Cookman College.

John C. Calhoun (1782–1850) was the seventh U.S. vice president (1825–1832).

Althea Gibson (1927–) was a tennis champion in the 1950s.

Dizzy Gillespie (1917–1993) was a jazz trumpeter and composer often referred to as the "King of Bebop."

DuBose Heyward (1885–1940) was an author. George Gershwin's opera *Porgy and Bess* (1935) was based on his novel *Porgy* (1925).

Andrew Jackson (1767–1845) was the seventh U.S. president (1829–1837) and a national military hero.

Jesse Jackson (1941–) is a minister and an African-American civil rights leader who founded the organization People United to Serve Humanity (PUSH).

Eartha Kitt (1928–) is a jazz and pop singer.

Strom Thurmond (1902–) was a powerful U.S. senator (1955–2003) and a supporter of states' rights. Thurmond (pictured above left) also served as governor of South Carolina.

William Westmoreland (1914–) commanded the U.S. forces in Vietnam (1964–1968) and was the U.S. Army chief of staff (1968–1972).

Vanna White (1957–) appears on the television show *Wheel of Fortune*.

Want to Know More?

At the Library

Britton, Tamara L. *The South Carolina Colony.* Edina, Minn.: Abdo Publishing, 2002.

Daise, Ronald, and Barbara McArtor (illustrator). *Little Muddy Waters: A Gullah Folk Tale.* Orangeburg, S.C.: Sandlapper, 1997.

Freeden, Charles. *South Carolina.* Minneapolis: Lerner, 2002.

Joseph, Paul. *South Carolina.* Minneapolis: Abdo & Daughters, 1998.

Weatherly, Myra. *South Carolina.* Danbury, Conn.: Children's Press, 2002.

On the Web

SClway

http://www.sciway.net
For maps, fun facts, and tourist information

South Carolina

http://www.myscgov.com
For the state web site, with information on South Carolina's history, government, economy, and events

South Carolina Department of Archives and History

http://www.state.sc.us/histro.html
For links to state history, facts, symbols, museums, and much more

Welcome to South Carolina

http://www.discoversouthcarolina.com
For a look at South Carolina's events, activities, parks, and sights

Through the Mail

South Carolina Department of Archives and History

8301 Parklane Road
Charleston, SC 29223
For information on South Carolina's history

South Carolina Department of Parks, Recreation & Tourism

1205 Pendleton Street
Columbia, SC 29201
For information on travel and interesting sights in South Carolina

On the Road

South Carolina State House

Gervais and Main Streets
Columbia, SC 29201
803/734-2430
To visit the state capitol

South Carolina State Museum

301 Gervais Street
Columbia, SC 29214
803/898-4921
To learn more about South Carolina's art, history, natural history, and science/technology

Index

African-Americans, 16, 20, 31, 32

Albemarle Pointe, 13

American Indians. *See* Native Americans.

Anderson, 25

animal life, 4, 10, 11, 36

Appalachian Mountains, 6

architecture, 36

art, 30

auto racing, 34

Bartram, William, 4

Blessing of the Fleet ceremony, 32

Blue Ridge Mountains, 7, 40

borders, 6, 40

Byrnes, James, 21

Calhoun, John C., 21

Carolina Colony, 14

Carolina Cup (horse race), 34

Catawba River, 13

Catawba tribe, 13, 31

Charleston, 9, 13, 16, 30, 32, 33, 35, 36

chemical manufacturing, 26

Cherokee tribe, 13, 40

Civil War, 16, 18, 35, 37

Clemson Tigers (football team), 33

Clemson University, 33

climate, 12

Coastal Plain, 8

coastline, 6, 8, 9, 10–11, 20, 36

colonists, 13, 14, 15, 39

Columbia, 23, 28, 30, 32, 37

Combahee River, 13

Confederate States of America, 16

Conroy, Pat, 30

culture, 31, 36, 38

Dickey, James, 30

Drayton Hall, 36

Edisto River, 13

executive branch of government, 22, 23

Fall Line, 7, 8

farming, 4, 8, 13, 14, 18, 19, 20, 25, 27, 39

Fighting Gamecocks (football team), 33

fishing industry, 32

forests, 10, 26

Fort Sumter, 16, 35

Gaffney, 39

Grand Strand, 9, 34

granite, 28

Great Depression, 19

Greenville, 7, 25, 30, 38

Gullah culture, 31, 36

Heyward, DuBose, 29

Hilton Head Island, 34, 36

insect life, 19

Jackson, Andrew, 16, 21

Johns, Jasper, 30

judicial branch of government, 22, 23

legislative branch of government, 22–23

literature, 29–30

local governments, 24. *See also* national government; state government.

manufacturing, 4, 19, 20, 25–26, 38

marine life, 4, 11, 32, 36

Middleton Place, 36

Military College of South Carolina, 33

mining, 28

Mount Pleasant, 32

mountains, 7, 12, 20, 40

music, 29

Myrtle Beach, 9, 32, 36

national government, 21. *See also* local governments; state government.

Native Americans, 13, 31

nullification, 16

Okra Strut Festival, 32

palmetto (state tree), 11

Peachoid, 39

Pee Dee River, 13

Piedmont region, 7, 19

plant life, 10–11, 19, 27, 32

plantations, 4, 14, 25, 30, 35, 36

population, 30

Poultry Festival, 32

Revolutionary War, 15–16, 39

Riverbanks Zoo, 37

rivers, 7, 13

Saint Helena Island, 31, 36

Sassafras Mountain, 40

Savannah River, 6

Sea Islands, 9, 31, 32, 36

Seafood Festival, 32

segregation, 16, 18, 20

service industries, 28

slavery, 14, 16, 30, 31

South Carolina State Fair, 32

South Carolina State Museum, 37

Southern 500 (auto-racing event), 34

Spartanburg, 7, 25, 38

Spoleto Festival, 32

sports, 33–34

state government, 22–23. *See also* local governments; national government.

State House, 23, 28, 37

state tree (palmetto), 11

statehood, 16

swamps, 11, 36

textile industry, 4, 19, 25, 26, 38

Thurmond, Strom, 21

timber industry, 26

tourism, 4, 9, 12, 20, 32, 36, 38

Townes, Charles, 37

University of South Carolina (USC), 33

Yamasee tribe, 13

About the Author

Ann Heinrichs grew up in Fort Smith, Arkansas, and lives in Chicago. She is the author of more than eighty books for children and young adults on Asian, African, and U.S. history and culture. Ann has also written numerous newspaper, magazine, and encyclopedia articles. She is an award-winning martial artist, specializing in t'ai chi empty-hand and sword forms.

Ann has traveled widely throughout the United States, Africa, Asia, and the Middle East. In exploring each state for this series, she rediscovered the people, history, and resources that make this a great land, as well as the concerns we share with people around the world.